SALISBURY TO YEOVIL

Vic Mitchell and Keith Smith

Cover picture: Since 1986 steam enthusiasts of the South have been treated to a number of special trips from Salisbury to both Yeovil Junction and Eastleigh - even to Exeter on rare occasions. With headboard to match its name, a magnificently presented Bulleid Pacific adorns platform 5 at Salisbury on 4th June 1987. (S.C.Nash)

First published September 1992

ISBN 1 873793 06 5

Typesetting   - Barbara Mitchell
Design   - Deborah Goodridge

Published by Middleton Press
              Easebourne Lane
              Midhurst
              West Sussex
              GU29 9AZ
              Tel: (0730) 813169

Printed & bound by Biddles Ltd,
              Guildford and Kings Lynn

CONTENTS

ACKNOWLEDGEMENTS

Our deep gratitude must be expressed to many of the photographers named in the captions and also to D.Brown, Dr.E.Course, G.Croughton, K.Deakin, J.B.Horne, P.Horne, Dr.S.Huber, N.Langridge, A.Ll.Lambert, R.Randell, D.Salter, N.Stanyon, C.Wilson and especially our wives.

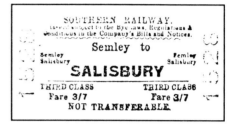

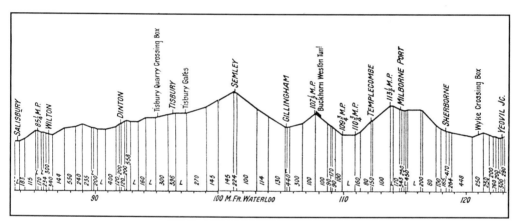

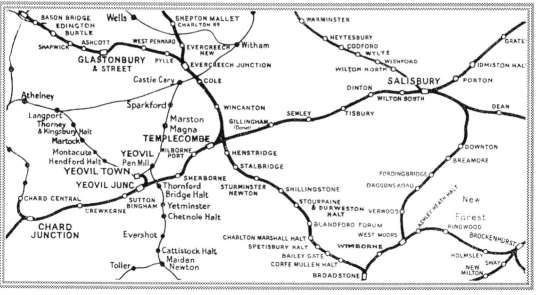

1955 route map.

GEOGRAPHICAL SETTING

Salisbury is at the confluence of the Avon and Nadder Rivers, the route following the valley of the latter to Tisbury. The chalk mass of Salisbury Plain flanks the line as far as Dinton, after which it passes successively over Upper Greensand, Purbeck Beds and Portland Beds, the last two of which include limestone deposits. This material was of economic importance at Tisbury.

From Tisbury to Semley, the line climbs up the valley of the River Sem to the summit, passing over Kimmeridge Clay for about ten miles. About one mile west of Gillingham it runs onto Coral Rag (clay and limestone) and climbs to a lesser summit before descending and crossing the clays of Blackmore Vale.

After rising to Templecombe the line traverses a variety of deposits including Limestone, Forest Marble and Fullers Earth. In the Sherborne area the predominant formation is Oolitic Limestone, this being the southern extension of the Cotswolds.

Yeovil Junction is built on the Yeovil Sands of the Yeo Valley which the line crosses at this location.

All maps are to the scale of 25" to 1 mile, unless otherwise indicated.

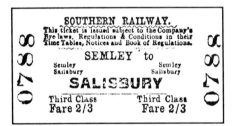

HISTORICAL BACKGROUND

Amongst the first railways in the area were the GWR-operated lines between Castle Cary and Weymouth and between Warminster and Salisbury, all having been opened in 1856-57.

The Salisbury & Yeovil Railway Co. secured its Act in 1854. The line through Salisbury Tunnel to Gillingham came into use on 2nd May 1859. The lines to Salisbury (Milford) from the east opened earlier, that from Eastleigh (Bishopstoke) in 1847 and the route from Andover in 1857. All these routes were operated by the London & South Western Railway. The extension from Gillingham to Sherborne took place on 7th May 1860 and to Yeovil (Hendford) on 1st June 1860 (goods on 1st September). Here it met the GWR's 1853 branch from Taunton end on. Hendford

station was superseded by Yeovil Town on 1st June 1861. All intermediate stations opened with the line.

Yeovil Junction and the line to Exeter first saw traffic on 19th July 1860, only five weeks after the direct line to Yeovil Town had opened. That connection was closed on 1st January 1870, Town station being served by a shuttle service from the Junction (until 2nd October 1966).

The route became part of the Southern Railway in 1923 and the Southern Region of British Railways in 1948. It was transferred to the Western Region in 1963 and became part of Network SouthEast in 1986, although Tisbury to Gillingham had been returned to the Southern Region in 1981.

PASSENGER SERVICES

Although the route opened in stages, the early timetables showed five weekday and two Sunday trains, a pattern that prevailed for over ten years.

The table below reveals the remarkably consistent service offered for so long, except in the world wars.

	Weekdays		Sundays
	Stopping	Fast	
1881	5	4	3
1890	5	4	3
1906	9	9	5
1914	11	6	4
1917	9	3	3
1924	7	5	5
1934	8	5	5
1944	5	6	6
1954	7	7	8
1965	6	9	10
1975	9	-	6
1985	13	-	9

For many years local stopping services were worked either side of Templecombe, these reaching their maximum in the 1940s, when there were five each way, each side.

Since 1967 there has been a regular basic two-hour interval timetable on the route, as trains had to be integrated into the then new electric services on the Bournemouth-Waterloo route. A feature of recent timetables has been an afternoon return working between Portsmouth & Southsea and Sherborne but this was withdrawn in January 1991, along with the long standing, but infrequent, West of England-Brighton service.

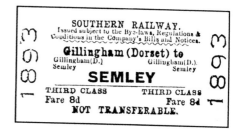

SOUTHERN RAILWAY.
Issued subject to the Bye-laws, Regulations & Conditions in the Company's Bills and Notices.
Gillingham (Dorset) to
Gillingham(D.) Gillingham(D.)
Semley Semley
SEMLEY
THIRD CLASS THIRD CLASS
Fare 8d Fare 8d
NOT TRANSFERABLE.
8931 / 1893

THROUGH TRAINS WATERLOO & SALISBURY TO YEOVIL JUNCTION & EXETER

WEEKDAYS (except Saturdays until 3 Oct)

			SX Y	S0 Y		RC	B RC	RX		RX		RX		SX RC	S0 BC		RX	
Waterloo 63	dep.	0140	....	0638	0638	....	0908	....	1108	1308	1508	....	1700	1708	....	19 08	
Woking 63	dep.		....	0708	0708	....	0935	....	1135	1335	1535	....	1730	1735	....	19 35	
Basingstoke 63	dep.		....	0731	0731	....	1000	....	1200	1400	1600	....	1756	1800	....	20 00	
Andover 63	dep.	0258	....	0750	0750	....	1019	....	1219	1419	1619	....	1816	1819	....	20 19	
Salisbury	dep.	0333	.... 06 52	0813	0813	....	1046	1120	1246	 1446	1646	....	1846	1846	....	20 46	
Tisbury	arr.			0830	0830												
Gillingham	arr.	0400	07 20	0843	0843	....	1112	1149	1312	 1515	1704	....	1904	1904	....	21 04	
Sherborne	arr.	0422	07 38	0901	0901	....	1130	....	1330	1535	1717	....	1917	1917	....	21 17	
Yeovil Junction	arr.	0433	07 48	0910	0910	....	1138	1211	1339	 1545	1745	....	1945	1945	....	21 35	
Crewkerne	arr.		08 00	0923	0923	....			1351	1557	1757	....			....	21 45	
Axminster	arr.		08 18	0939	0946	....	1202	1235	1407	 1613	1813	....	2013	2013	....	21 57	
Honiton	arr.		08 33	0955	1002	....	1218	1256	1425	 1632	1835	....	2035	2035	....	22 13	
Whimple	arr.		08 42	1004	1011	....				1642		....			....	22 29	
Exeter Central	arr.		08/53	1018	1025	....	1236	1314	1445	 1654	1854	....	2054	2054	....	22 49	
Exeter St Davids	arr.		09 14	1025	1032	....	1242	1320	1454	 1700	1902	....	2100	2100	....	22055	

SATURDAYS until 3 Oct · SUNDAYS

				Y BC	V BC	RC	RC		B BC	RC	BC	BC		Z BZ	BC		BC	
Waterloo 63	dep.	0140	....	0638	08(00	09 00	....	1100	1300	1500	1700	1900	0130	.... 09(08	1108	....	1608	 1908
Woking 63	dep.		....	0708	08(31	09 30	....	1130	1330	1530	1730	1930		.... 09(35	1135	....	1635	 1935
Basingstoke 63	dep.		....	0731	08(57	09 57	....	1157	1357	1557	1757	1957		.... 10(00	1200	....	1700	 2000
Andover 63	dep.	0258	....	0750	09(18	10 18	....	1218	1418	1618	1818	2018	0313	.... 10(19	1219	....	1719	 2019
Salisbury	dep.	0333	.... 06 52	0813	09 44	10 46	1120	1246	1446	1646	1846	2046	0400	.... 10 46	1246	....	1746	 2046
Tisbury	arr.			0830					1704	1904	2104							
Gillingham	arr.	0400	07 20	0843	.()	11 12	1149	1312	1515	1717	1917	2117	0448	.... 11 12	1312	....	1812	 2112
Sherborne	arr.	0422	07 38	0901	.(09(23	11 24	....	1330	1535	1735	1935	2135	0509	.... 11 29	1329	....	1829	 2129
Yeovil Junction	arr.	0433	07 48	0910	10 33	11 33	1211	1339	1545	1745	1945	2145	0518	.... 11 39	1339	....	1839	 2139
Crewkerne	arr.		08 00	0923	10 45	....			1351	1557	1757	1957	2157		.... 11 51	1351	 1851	 2151
Axminster	arr.		08 18	0947	11 13	12 12	1235	1407	1613	1813	2013	2213		.... 12/07	1407	....	1917	 2207
Honiton	arr.		08 33	1002	11 30	12 18	1256	1425	1632	1835	2035	2229		.... 12/24	1424	....	1932	 2224
Whimple	arr.		08 42	1012	.(													
Exeter Central	arr.		08 53	1024	11 50	12 39	1314	1445	1654	1854	2054	2249		.... 12/44	1444	....	1949	 2244
Exeter St Davids	arr.		09H04	1030	11 56	12 48	1320	1454	1700	1900	2100	2255		.... 12/50	1450	....	1955	 2244

B From or to Brighton
BC Buffet service
BZ Buffet service until 6 Sept
C 3 Oct only
f Departs 0921
H Arrives 0924 on 3 Oct

Q Saturdays only. On Mons to Fris connection arrives 2310
RC Restaurant car
RX Restaurant car Mons to Fris; buffet service Saturdays

S0 Saturdays only
SX Mondays to Fridays
V 13 June to 5 Sept
Y Calls Surbiton at 0654
Z Until 4 Oct

1970 timetable

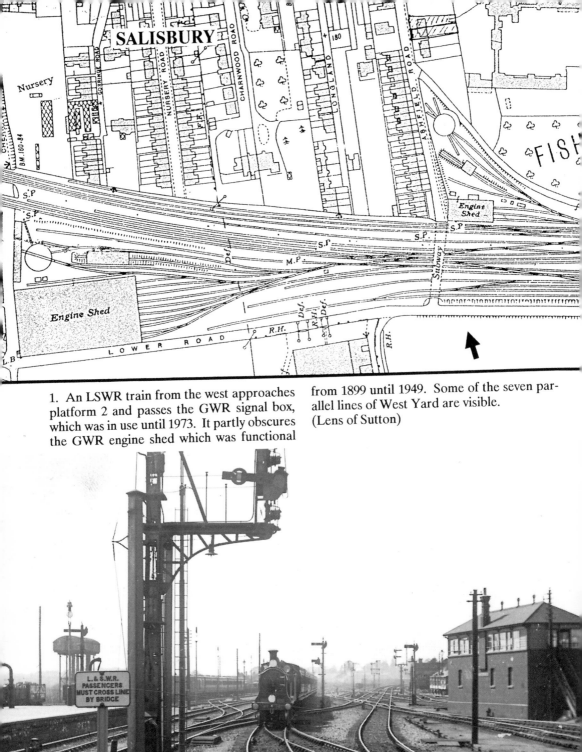

1. An LSWR train from the west approaches platform 2 and passes the GWR signal box, which was in use until 1973. It partly obscures the GWR engine shed which was functional from 1899 until 1949. Some of the seven parallel lines of West Yard are visible. (Lens of Sutton)

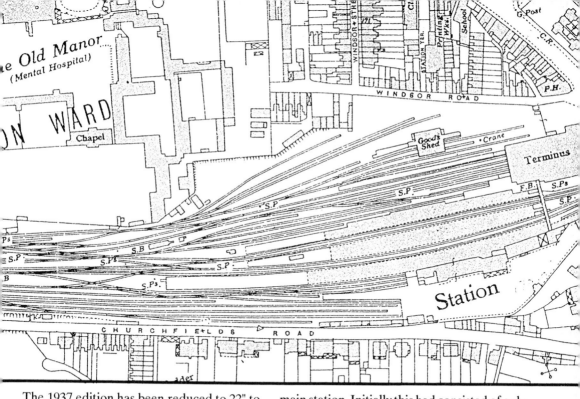

The 1937 edition has been reduced to 22" to 1 mile in order to include the former GWR terminus (top right) and the ex-LSWR engine shed (lower left). The GWR's engine shed is left of centre. Its terminus closed on 12th September 1932, after which date its trains ran into one of the four through platforms of the main station. Initially this had consisted of only one platform on the down side and up trains usually had to reverse into it. In 1878 an up platform was built, sited beyond the right border of the map. Extensive rebuilding took place in 1900-02 to provide the present platforms.

2. Salisbury was in the headlines on 1st July 1906 when the driver of a boat train from Plymouth failed to observe the 30mph speed limit and raced through at more than double the speed. His high-boilered class L12 rolled over and hit another engine which prevented it falling into Fisherton Street. The canopy of the up bay platform (no. 6) is in the background. The crew were among the 28 who lost their lives. (Lens of Sutton)

3. The building on the left has been used for many years by carriage examiners, originally having been used also for heating foot warmers. In earlier years a transfer shed had stood nearby which contained a GWR broad gauge siding parallel to an LSWR standard gauge one. Between them stood a platform for the transfer of goods traffic. (D.Cullum coll.)

London & South Western Ry
SHIPWRECKED MARINER
SOUTHAMPTON to
CARDIFF
Via Sarum Bristol & Sev'n Tunnel
Soton   Soton
Cardiff   Cardiff
THIRD   (S.1)   THIRD
CLASS   See over   CLASS
Fare 5/1¾   Fare 5/1¾

9779

4. No. 21C1 *Channel Packet* was the first of the "Merchant Navy" class and is seen on 29th June 1946, when it still retained its full air-smoothing panels between its buffers and outside cylinders. Until 6th February 1950 London- Exeter expresses generally changed engines here. (C.L.Caddy coll.)

5. One of the first tasks of the new British Railways Board when it was formed in 1948 was to conduct locomotive trials before establishing standard designs. Ex-LMSR "Royal Scot" no. 46154 waits to leave with the 10.50am from Waterloo on 15th June of that year. Also visible is the dynamometer car for recording its performance, class N15 no. 454 *Queen Guinevere* and the station pilot, class M7 0-4-4T no. 248. (J.R.W.Kirkby)

IT IS LEAVING. STEAM SANDERS ON

6. The 11.49am Yeovil Junction to Salisbury stopping train was hauled by class H15 no. 30330 on 19th August 1951. The former 93-lever GWR signal box had been designated "C" soon after nationalisation. The LSWR had pioneered pneumatic signalling and point operation - hence the large trackside boxes. Both "A" (East) and "B" (West) boxes had 64 levers operating air compressed at only 15 psi. (N.Sprinks)

7. The 10.12 am Brighton to Plymouth was headed by no. 34089 *602 Squadron* on 7th August 1965, as the rostered diesel locomotive had failed. Salisbury "B" box (right) dates from 1926 when it was fitted with electro-pneumatic equipment. (S.C.Nash)

8. Prior to the end of steam traction in July 1967 a number of specials were operated. This is the "A2 Commemorative Railtour" on 14th August 1966, featuring class A2 no. 60532 *Blue Peter*. Despite its pristine condition, one photographer preferred the female form. Note the ex-GWR perforated signal arm. (R.E.Ruffell)

9. On 6th December 1980, a Plymouth to Paddington train was diverted at Westbury to run via Salisbury and Basingstoke. It made an unusual sight in the company of an SR signal operated by an LSWR pneumatic cylinder as it entered platform 2.
(J.S.Petley)

NEVER. IT IS SHUNTING FROM PLTFM 2 OVER TO THE DOWN M.L. SEE DUMMY OFF

10. The first station building is on the right and is still standing, its former parcel office accommodating the signalling panel since 1981. The main building was erected prior to the platform alterations of 1900-02 and is seen in 1973, along with vintage telephone boxes. (J.Scrace)

11. The signal shown in picture 9 is seen on 2nd July 1981 as it nears the end of its life. The replacement is seen above no. 31159 as it heads west with ballast. On the left is the depot of Rail Ambassador Exhibition Trains, who had to vacate the premises to make way for a new £7m "Traincare Depot" for class 159 Turbos which was built in 1992. (J.S.Petley)

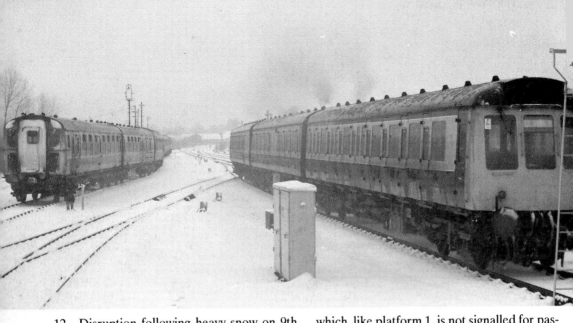

12. Disruption following heavy snow on 9th February 1985 resulted in the 10.10 Portsmouth Harbour service being worked by a DMU. Lower left is the line to platform 5 which, like platform 1, is not signalled for passenger trains. The adjacent siding is also used for stock berthing. (C.Hall)

13. Everyone stopped to stare on 24th January 1986 as three new class 59 locomotives from General Motors were hauled through platform 3 en route from Southampton Docks to their owners' depot at Merehead. Foster Yeoman were the first firm to operate a fleet of locomotives on BR. (A.Dasi-Sutton)

14. The 1980s saw a remarkable revival of occasional steam trains between Salisbury and Yeovil Junction, some journeys originating at Eastleigh. In the summer of 1992 there were some trips to Exeter also. Class A4 no. 4498 *Sir Nigel Gresley* is seen in light steam on 18th October 1986. (P.G.Barnes)

15. Class 155 Sprinters replaced locomotive hauled MkIs on the Brighton / Portsmouth - Cardiff services in May 1988, the combined units of such a service being seen on 6th April 1991. Combination of units at Fareham ceased in May 1992, resulting in a more frequent service through Salisbury. By that date class 158 air conditioned Sprinters were universal on the route. (P.G.Barnes)

SALISBURY SHED

16. The first engine shed had three roads and was sited near the west end of the present platform 4. A second shed of similar size was built close by in 1885, on land now occupied by the car park. Both sheds were lost in the 1901 rebuilding. The roof of the original down platform is behind the chimney of *Python*, one of the "Centaur" class built in 1868. "SWR" lettering was applied from 1895 to 1897 only. (E.W.Fry coll.)

17. The new shed had ten roads and a slate roof on five spans. On the right is the elevated coal stage and in the background is the enginemen's dormitory, surmounted by a water tank. On shed on 30th April 1928 are class L11 4-4-0 no. E411 and class 0395 0-6-0 no. E083. (H.C.Casserley)

SOUTHERN RAILWAY.
Issued subject to the Bye-Laws, Regulations & Conditions in the Company's Bills and Notices.

Salisbury to

Salisbury
Waterloo

Salisbury
Waterloo

WATERLOO
Via Oakley

THIRD CLASS
Fare 12/10
NOT TRANSFERABLE.

THIRD CLASS
Fare 12/10

6074

6074

18. Seen on the same day are nos. E650, E656 and E645, all of class A12. At this time, the shed was allocated over 60 locomotives for working principally to London, Bournemouth, Exeter and Portsmouth. (H.C.Casserley)

19. The water softener column is evident as part of the fleet simmer in the sun on 31st May 1929. Included are nos. E162 (G6), E148 (L11), E755 (N15) and E512 (S15). The 55ft turntable had been replaced by one of 65ft length in about 1912. (H.C.Casserley)

20. The shed was reroofed with corrugated asbestos in November 1954 and remained in use until the end of steam in July 1967. It continued to serve as a signing-on point until February 1969. Seen on 3rd April 1965 are no. 34100 *Appledore*, class 5 no. 73087 *Linette*, class 4 no. 76009 and class U no. 31790. The site was cleared without delay. (S.C.Nash)

WEST OF SALISBURY

21. Viewed from Skew Bridge, which carries the A30, two class 158 Sprinters pass one another while working between Portsmouth Harbour and Cardiff on 13th April 1991. Until 27th October 1973 Western Region trains ran on separate parallel tracks, where trees grow on the left of this picture. The 404ft cathedral spire is the tallest in England. (P.G.Barnes)

22. Nearly two miles west of Salisbury, part of the former Western Region track was retained to give access to the ECC Quarrys' sidings at Quidhampton, which were opened on 18th November 1973. Chalk slurry is loaded for conveyance to Port Elphinstone near Aberdeen. There it is used to help make paper as white as this page. This is the view towards Wilton on 24th September 1991, by which time the train ran, thrice weekly. (M.Turvey)

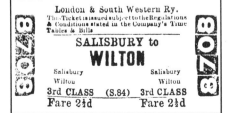

London & South Western Ry.
This Ticket is issued subject to the Regulations
& Conditions stated in the Company's Time
Tables & Bills
SALISBURY to
WILTON
Salisbury   Salisbury
Wilton   Wilton
3rd CLASS (S.84)   3rd CLASS
Fare 2½d   Fare 2½d

23. The Yeovil and Westbury routes now diverge two miles from Salisbury and run parallel for about a quarter of a mile before parting near Wilton. Red liveried no. 47717 is passing under Devizes Road on 20th July 1991 with the 07.52 from Waterloo, running 30 minutes late. (P.G.Barnes)

WILTON SOUTH

24. Once the capital town of Wessex but now eclipsed by Salisbury, Wilton has a market house dating from 1738 and many other historic buildings, notably Wilton House. The county of Wiltshire took its name from Wilton. Visitors and local residents once generated a considerable traffic. The suffix "South" was added on 26th September 1949. (Lens of Sutton)

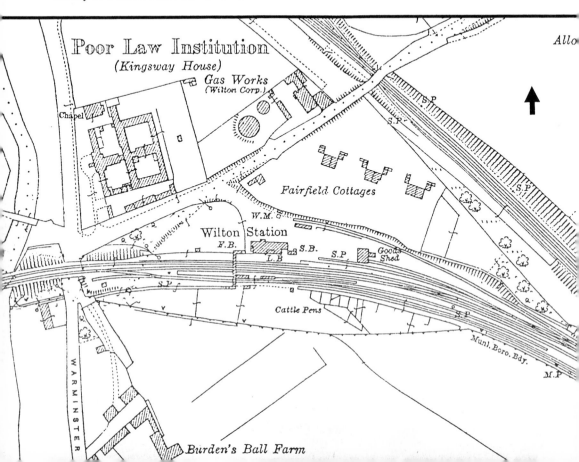

25. While a porter displays one empty barrow, the other bears a roll of carpet, presumably from the nearby world-famous carpet factory. The town was once the centre of the wool trade for a large district. Note the footbridge extension on the left. (Lens of Sutton)

The 1925 edition has part of the GWR station's sidings at the top. Although only having a population of about 2000 at this time, Wilton was a municipal borough and Wilton Corporation had a gasworks (centre). This and the adjacent workhouse would have required rail-borne coal in quantity. Top to bottom on the left is the River Wylye and Warminster Road (A36).

26. Class U1 no. 1894 was working the stopping train from Yeovil Junction to Salisbury on 20th July 1937 when it was recorded near the typical early LSWR signal box. This box controlled Wilton Junction from 1973 until 1981, when Salisbury panel took over. The box is now in use at Medstead & Four Marks on the Mid-Hants Railway. (H.C.Casserley)

27. Many LSWR stations were slate-hung as damp penetration was common in the absence of cavity walls. The passenger coach was probably a cripple, abandoned in the siding to be photographed on 5th July 1963. The crane to the right of the shed was rated at two tons capacity. (H.C.Casserley)

Wilton South	1928	1936
No. of passenger tickets issued	2480	917
No. of season tickets issued	10	3
No. of tickets collected	3051	1687
No. of telegrams	1990	816
Parcels forwarded	1949	1643
Parcels received	4621	4760
Horses forwarded	120	69
Cans of milk forwarded	25667	-
Cans of milk received	2	-
General goods forwarded (tons)	1516	862
General goods received (tons)	1714	1157
Coal, Coke etc.	1223	345
Other minerals forwarded	218	624
Other minerals received	1298	2711
Trucks livestock forwarded	246	87
Trucks livestock received	74	5
Lavatory pennies	120	83

28. A 1964 photograph includes the former workhouse and the down siding. The latter was used for many years for changing the engines of the down "Devon Belle". This avoided having to stop for water at Salisbury, which was time consuming. There were no water troughs on the SR. (C.L.Caddy)

29. Goods services ceased on 6th July 1964 and the station was closed to passengers on 7th March 1966, in which year the sidings were lifted. The north elevation was pictured in 1975. The line west of Wilton was singled on 2nd April 1967. (J.Scrace)

L.&.S.W.R.

SALISBURY TO

WORTHING

THIRD CLASS PARLIAMENTARY

The Connection of Trains Not
Guaranteed. (See Back)
(Worthing) (Worthing)

AU.14 N76   800

SOUTHERN RAILWAY.
This ticket is issued subject to the Company's
Bye-laws, Regulations & Conditions in their
Time Tables, Notices and Book of Regulations.
Available on DAY of issue ONLY

Salisbury to

Salisbury   Salisbury
Yeovil Town   Yeovil Town

YEOVIL TOWN

Via Yeovil Junc.

Third Class   Third Class
Fare 5/2   Fare 5/2

6871   6871

30. The main buildings were still standing as the 13.10 Waterloo to Exeter passed on 16th October 1986, the down platform having long gone. No. 50025 *Invincible* was not living up to its name, as it required assistance from no. 33005. The ageing class 50s acquired a bad reputation for reliability on the route, the succeeding class 47s eventually gaining the same distinction. (J.S.Petley)

DINTON

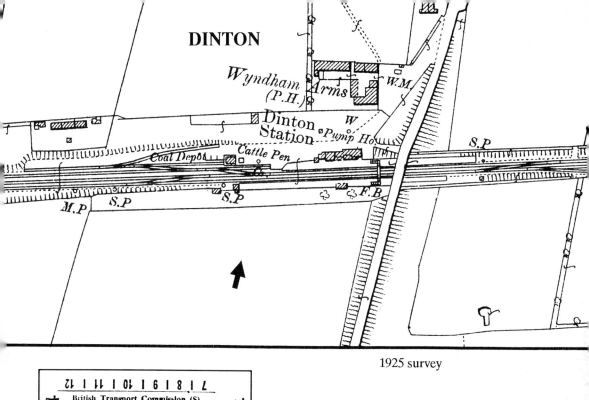

Wyndham Arms
(P.H.)

W.M.

Dinton
Station

W
Pump Ho

S.P

Coal Depot

Cattle Pen

M.P   S.P

S.P

S.P

F.B

1925 survey

British Transport Commission (S)
DINTON
PLATFORM TICKET 1d.
Available one hour on day of issue only.
Not valid in trains.   Not transferable.
To be given up when leaving platform
For conditions see over

1014

1014

31. The village had a population of under 600 throughout the life of the station, which closed to passengers on 7th March 1966 and to goods on 18th April following. As suggested by the fleet of barrows, local produce was an important source of revenue. (Lens of Sutton)

32. Milk churns and a chicken coop near the 5-ton crane confirm the agricultural nature of traffic here between the wars. The summer house type building on the up platform was probably the first signal box. The second is on the left. (Lens of Sutton)

33. At the height of World War I, a two mile long branch south to Fovant Camp was built. It was in use intermittently between 1916 and 1924. *Hampshire* is seen at the terminus, *Woolmer* and *Westminster* being its companions on this steep branch graded at mostly 1 in 35. (Lens of Sutton)

34. East of the station, on the up side, other sidings were in use in both World Wars to Baverstock Depot. In 1948 they served as a site for the dismantling of 38 SR locomotives. (J.H.Aston)

Dinton	1928	1936
No. of passenger tickets issued	7067	1979
No. of season tickets issued	37	24
No. of tickets collected	7933	2816
No. of telegrams	929	11
Parcels forwarded	769	686
Parcels received	2607	2060
Horses forwarded	20	-
Milk forwarded - cans 1928/gallons1936	55956	127690
Milk received - cans 1928/gallons 1936	16	59
General goods forwarded (tons)	2730	204
General goods received (tons)	1354	960
Coal, Coke etc.	2674	1827
Other minerals forwarded	353	251
Other minerals received	1970	471
Trucks livestock forwarded	148	19
Trucks livestock received	24	39
Lavatory pennies	132	106

35. The third box was opened on 8th November 1942 and is seen here in 1964 as no. 34101 *Hartland* runs east. The box had 32 levers. The military sidings were greatly expanded in connection with underground munition stores in 1942. (J.W.T.House/C.L.Caddy)

36. Seen in 1981, the substantial station house and buildings were well maintained. A stores van (extreme right) and an office for a senior railman were in use in connection with Ministry of Defence traffic. (D.Cullum)

38. South of the station, new sidings were brought into use on 10th July 1938 to serve the Dinton Depot of the RAF. These were laid on part of the site of the Fovant Military Railway and included exchange sidings with a 2ft. gauge system, as at Chilmark. Since 1967, access was by means of a ground frame (far right) but, by the early 1990s, the sidings were seldom used. (P.G.Barnes)

37. A Rolls Royce engined MOD Sentinel approaches the station on 7th August 1981 on the former up line, which, after the 1967 singling, was retained to link the Baverstock sidings (ex-Admiralty) to the east, with the Chilmark sidings (ex-RAF) to the west of the station. Disused limestone mines near Chilmark, which once provided material for the construction of Salisbury Cathedral, were chosen as a site for RAF bomb storage in 1937. Ultimately there were 2½ miles of standard gauge track, the 2ft gauge lines totalling nine miles. Running on the latter in 1976 were 95 wagons, one bogie coach, six rock fall rescue wagons, two fire tenders, four Baguely-Drewry diesels and three battery electrics from the same maker, together with three redundant Ruston & Hornsby diesels. Air Ministry control passed to the Ministry of Defence in 1964. In 1992, there were two standard gauge diesels operating, together with seven locomotives of narrow gauge. (D.Cullum)

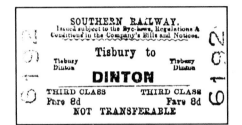

SOUTHERN RAILWAY.
Issued subject to the Bye-laws, Regulations &
Conditions in the Company's Bills and Notices.

Tisbury to

Tisbury   Tisbury
Dinton   Dinton

DINTON

THIRD CLASS   THIRD CLASS
Fare 8d   Fare 8d

NOT TRANSFERABLE

6162

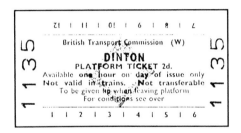

British Transport Commission (W)

DINTON

PLATFORM TICKET 2d.

Available one hour on day of issue only
Not valid in trains. Not transferable
To be given up when leaving platform
For conditions see over

7 8 9 10 11 12

1 2 3 4 5 6

1135   1135

39. This and the previous picture were taken on 20th July 1991, this view showing the re-painted D400 with the 10.20 from Exeter St. Davids. The trees in the left of this view are on the right of the previous one. The line to Chilmark is to the right of the train. (P.G.Barnes)

WEST OF DINTON

40. An eastward view from 1991 shows the unusual Teffont Mill crossing, half a mile west of the station. Trains on the main line (right) operate miniature red and green lights on the roadway but those on the Chilmark siding (left) have to stop so that a crew member can operate the lights by means of a plunger. (J.Scrace)

41. Following the automation of other crossings, Tisbury Quarry became user operated on 1st March 1967, with red and green indicator lights. This view is from 1981, the location being about three miles west of Dinton. (D.Cullum)

42. A northward view includes the cattle pens, the 5-ton crane and the long waiting shelters. In 1901 there were under 1500 inhabitants but the rural district included 7700. (Lens of Sutton)

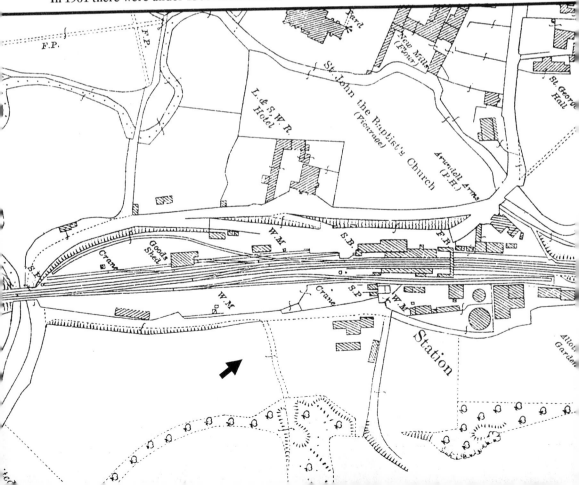

43. A shadow reveals that the down starter is off for the 3.5pm Salisbury to Exeter Central to depart on 26th June 1948. Class N15 no. 30744 has its BR number on the buffer beam - this was not to be BR standard practice; cast smokebox numberplates soon became universal. (J.H.Aston)

←—————

The 1925 edition includes circles which indicate the gas holders of the rail served gasworks. New Mills was formerly Wiltshire Brewery, which was probably unable to compete with rail borne beer from the big producers. Unusually, there are three weighing machines (W.M.) and two cranes. The River Sem meanders across the map.

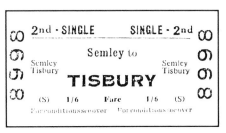

44. When photographed in September 1964 the footbridge had lost its cover, and a new signal box had appeared. This was opened on 12th October 1958. Goods facilities were withdrawn on 18th April 1966 and the down line and sidings were lifted in 1967. (C.L.Caddy)

45. A 1981 view from the river bridge reveals that the station was still intact but does not show that the down platform had been removed following the singling of 1967. (D.Cullum)

46. Another 1981 picture shows that Chantry Path still crossed the line on the level, giving direct access to the site of the ancient castle ditches. The 19 miles between Wilton and Gillingham, devoid of a passing place, was a great operational handicap and compounded delays when late running occurred. (D.Cullum)

47. The signal box closed on 5th February 1967 and is seen in September 1988. A passing loop was opened on 24th March 1986 in an attempt to improve timekeeping. This had to be sited east of the station as the land on the right had been sold. The junction signal at the far end of the platform shows that it was available for bidirectional running, controlled from Salisbury panel. (J.Scrace)

Tisbury	1928	1936
No. of passenger tickets issued	15257	6591
No. of season tickets issued	110	86
No. of tickets collected	18642	10065
No. of telegrams	1043	990
Parcels forwarded	2930	1658
Parcels received	8885	10470
Horses forwarded	46	36
Milk forwarded - cans 1928/gallons1936	57827	93379
Milk received - cans 1928/gallons 1936	62	59
General goods forwarded (tons)	3632	348
General goods received (tons)	5172	3682
Coal, Coke etc.	6278	6307
Other minerals forwarded	1450	655
Other minerals received	5974	395
Trucks livestock forwarded	47	5
Trucks livestock received	88	84
Lavatory pennies	252	319

48. One mile west of Tisbury is Tisbury Gates, which was renamed Tisbury West Level Crossing. A box was built here in 1892 and reduced to a ground frame in 1922. The box seen here in 1991 is not in the original position and is privately owned. (P.G.Barnes)

8710   SOUTHERN RAILWAY.
ADMIT
ONE MOTOR CAR or OTHER VEHICLE
TO BE PARKED IN THE
STATION APPROACH AT
GILLINGHAM (Dorset)
CHARGE 6d
FOR CONDITIONS SEE BACK.
8710

SEMLEY

49. The station was situated half a mile north-east of the small village and was a centre for agricultural traffic, notably milk. Like most other stations on the route, the footbridge was roofed and fully glazed. (Lens of Sutton)

50. Milk churns were largely displaced by bulk rail tankers in 1931, these running until 1980. The LSWR provided facilities for a wholesale milk depot at Semley in 1874. By 1890 London was receiving 84% of its milk by rail from a variety of sources. This westward view is from 1928. (H.C.Casserley)

51. The milk factory chimney is evident in this 1955 photograph. The factory drew electricity from the grid from 1932 onwards and in consequence coal traffic at the station declined that year. The 5-ton crane is obscured by the goods shed. (D.Cullum)

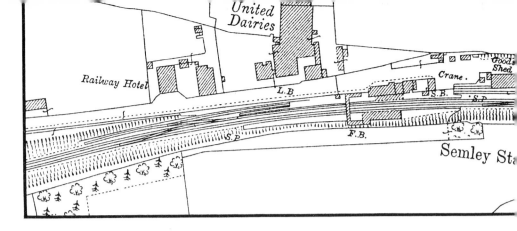

1925 edition

52. The new signal box is seen shortly after its opening, which took place on 29th January 1961. No. 34052 *Lord Dowding* waits with a stopping train while the fireman builds his fire at the summit of the line.
(J.W.T.House/C.L.Caddy)

53. By 2nd June 1963 the signalman had graduated from a motorcycle to a Hillman Husky, and the footbridge had lost its weather protection. Improvements included crossing illumination and platform lengthening.
(C.L.Caddy) MIGHT BE A DIFFERENT SIGNALMAN

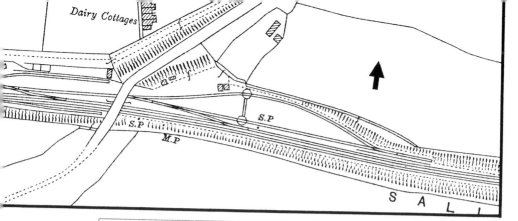

Semley	1928	1936
No. of passenger tickets issued	13531	6906
No. of season tickets issued	20	14
No. of tickets collected	17031	13462
No. of telegrams	4525	2341
Parcels forwarded	22126	13311
Parcels received	17263	19331
Horses forwarded	196	110
Milk forwarded - cans 1928/gallons1936	83165	4780186
Milk received - cans 1928/gallons 1936	1275	2500
General goods forwarded (tons)	946	1056
General goods received (tons)	4895	2772
Coal, Coke etc.	6976	4332
Other minerals forwarded	135	109
Other minerals received	2228	1166
Trucks livestock forwarded	201	181
Trucks livestock received	104	89
Lavatory pennies	396	473

54. Goods services were withdrawn on 5th April 1965 and passenger closure followed on 7th March 1966. This photograph was taken on 1st May following, the sign removers being fully occupied elsewhere at that period. (C.L.Caddy)

55. Following closure, the buildings were retained and protected by railings owing to the new elevation of the roadway. Only the former down line remained in use. (C.Hall)

GILLINGHAM

From the 1934 appendix.

56. The route crosses from Wiltshire to Dorset before reaching Gillingham, which is pronounced with a hard "G" to distinguish it from the Kent town of the same spelling. The National Stud was situated near here before being moved to Newmarket. William Tite's impressive architecture can be seen at many stations from here to Exeter. (Lens of Sutton)

57. Milk churns in profusion await the van train approaching. Churns are also evident in the goods yard, as is the 5-ton crane. The LSWR operated a bus service to Mere, Zeals and Shaftesbury from this station. (Lens of Sutton)

58. Unlike the less used stations further east, the footbridge here does not seem to have been roofed. The population of the town remained at about 4000 for the first 100 years of the station's life. No. 560 was a class T3 4-4-0, in use from 1893 until 1932. (Lens of Sutton)

59. With a flower in his button hole, a member of staff studies dockets as a down stopping train approaches. The steel span and brick approaches to the footbridge were removed in 1967 and replaced by an all-concrete structure from Dinton. (Lens of Sutton)

60. Although poor quality, the picture is of interest as it includes the bacon factory and cheese factory (see map), both sources of railway revenue. Also noteworthy is the horse engaged in shunting and an up signal on the down side. Shunting by steam did nothing to enhance the fertility of the railwayman's lineside allotment. (Lens of Sutton)

Gillingham	1928	1936
No. of passenger tickets issued	23486	17307
No. of season tickets issued	7	8
No. of tickets collected	27563	22362
No. of telegrams	4556	3015
Parcels forwarded	25810	24007
Parcels received	20044	24510
Horses forwarded	312	130
Milk forwarded - cans 1928/gallons1936	20340	390529
Milk received - cans 1928/gallons 1936	119	49382
General goods forwarded (tons)	6525	3497
General goods received (tons)	14578	7804
Coal, Coke etc.	16208	14076
Other minerals forwarded	1573	857
Other minerals received	8584	911
Trucks livestock forwarded	368	137
Trucks livestock received	933	1872
Lavatory pennies	780	721

61. Looking west in September 1956, we see the tile and pottery works (earlier rail connected by means of a turntable), a new signal box under construction (into use on 28th April 1957), and a large locomotive close to the goods shed. (D.Cullum)

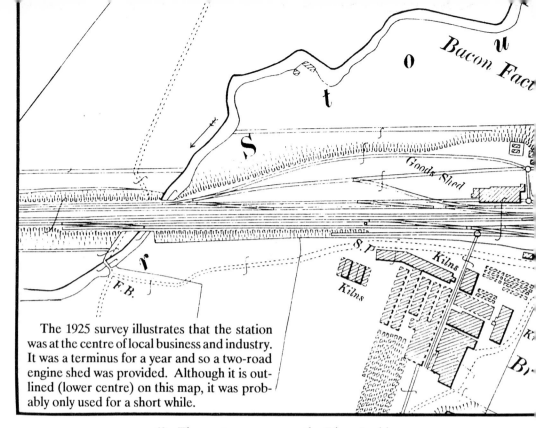

The map includes labels: *Bacon Fact...*, *Goods Shed*, *Kilns*, *S. P.*, *Kilns*, *F.B.*, and scattered letters *S*, *t*, *o*, *u*, *r*.

The 1925 survey illustrates that the station was at the centre of local business and industry. It was a terminus for a year and so a two-road engine shed was provided. Although it is outlined (lower centre) on this map, it was probably only used for a short while.

62. The route passes over the River Lodden east of the station and the River Stour west of it. Trains starting in either direction have a stiff climb. No. 34076 *41 Squadron* is accelerating west on 5th September 1964. (J.H.Bird)

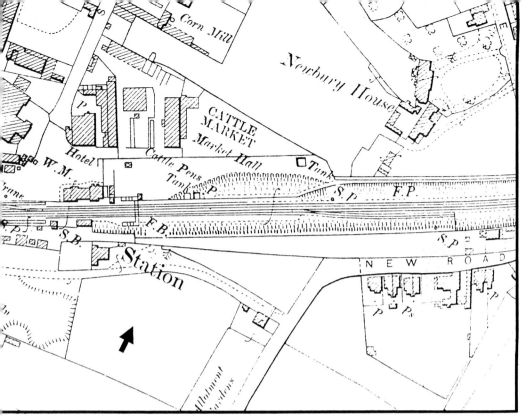

63. The exterior was recorded in October 1981, by which date most up trains ran to Waterloo. Until 1966 almost all services calling here terminated at Salisbury, except in the very early years. (D.Cullum)

64. The weighing machine was a feature of all but the smallest goods yard but was seldom photographed. This is the 15-ton model from Pooley & Son, who sent their mobile workshop van by goods train for regular maintenance and calibration of the equipment. (C.Hall)

65. General goods traffic ceased on 5th April 1965 but one up siding was retained to serve the Shellstar Fertiliser Depot (centre), later renamed UKF. In 1992 part of a train of bogie pallet vans usually arrived each week from Ince & Elton in Cheshire. The other part was left at Andover. This and the next picture were taken on 20th April 1991. (P.G.Barnes)

66. Until 1986 this was the only passing loop between Templecombe and Wilton. No. 33114 is leaving with the 12.25 from Exeter St. Davids (20 minutes late) and is on the up reversible line. Down trains use it when no passing is involved, passengers being saved the climb over the footbridge. (P.G.Barnes)

WEST OF GILLINGHAM

67. After climbing steeply for two miles from Gillingham, the line passes through the 742yd long Buckhorn Western Tunnel, also known as Gillingham Tunnel. Above it was the stud farm on the Sandley Estate, already mentioned. (Lens of Sutton)

68. Bound for West of England destinations, the train of Bulleid coaches bends as it passes over the summit in the summer of 1949. The smartly lined locomotive is no. 35024 *East Asiatic Company*, new in the previous year. (D.Cullum coll.)

SOUTHERN RAILWAY.
Issued subject to the Bye-laws, Regulations & Conditions in the Company's Bills and Notices.

Gillingham(Dorset) to
Gillingham(Dorset)   Gillingham(Dorset)
Semley   Semley

SEMLEY

THIRD CLASS   THIRD CLASS
Fare 11d.   Fare 11d.

NOT TRANSFERABLE

6228

69. Class 4 2-6-0 no. 76007 emerges from the western end of the tunnel on 5th September 1964, with a stopping train. The summit is about 350ft above sea level. (C.L.Caddy)

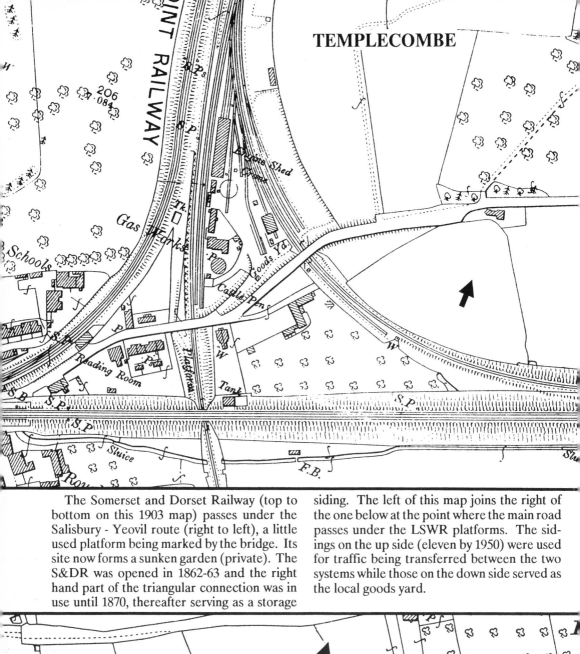

TEMPLECOMBE

The Somerset and Dorset Railway (top to bottom on this 1903 map) passes under the Salisbury - Yeovil route (right to left), a little used platform being marked by the bridge. Its site now forms a sunken garden (private). The S&DR was opened in 1862-63 and the right hand part of the triangular connection was in use until 1870, thereafter serving as a storage siding. The left of this map joins the right of the one below at the point where the main road passes under the LSWR platforms. The sidings on the up side (eleven by 1950) were used for traffic being transferred between the two systems while those on the down side served as the local goods yard.

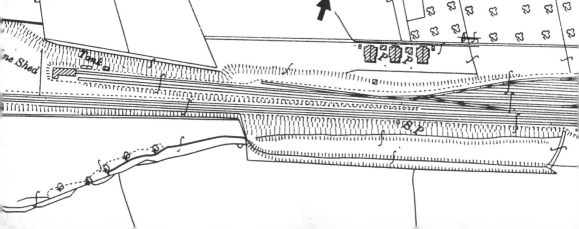

The first station on the S&D route (centre) had originally been the terminus of the Somerset Central Railway until its union with the Dorset Central Railway. Until 1867, the LSWR main line was single and a loop was provided (right) for the use of an LSWR operated shuttle service between the two stations. From 1867 until 1870 most S&D trains used this awkward route, replacing the shuttle. This involved running on the LSWR up line in both directions, a very unsatisfactory arrangement in those days of crude signalling. Thus the double tracked western curve came into use in 1870 and the lower station was largely abandoned, although a new low-level platform was built in about 1873. (Railway Magazine)

FROM WINCANTON

2ND LINE OPENED IN 1884

Nº 3 JUNCTION

Nº 2 JUNCTION

STATION IN 1861

BRUTON TO TEMPLECOMBE LINE ENDED HERE IN 1861

LAYOUT OF JUNCTION IN 1861

TO LONDON

NEW CONNECTING LINES OPENED IN 1870

RAILWAY

Nº 1 JUNCTION REMOVED IN JANUARY, 1887

GS LAID IN PRIOR TO 1866

SOUTHERN

TEMPLECOMBE TO BLANDFORD OPENED IN 1863

LOWER PLATFORM

OM EXETER TEMPLECOMBE

TO BLANDFORD

L a n e

Templecombe Junction

Templecombe Station

St. Mary's Ch.
(Rectory)

Weir

S.P.

S.P.

S.P.

S.P.

Goods Shed

Cattle Pens

Mission Hall

70. The far side of the up platform served S&D trains, both up and down, much reversing being required. There were many transfer freights passing that side of the station and large numbers of parcels etc. were moved across the platform. A subway was provided to the down platform and exit. (D.Cullum coll.)

> **Our** *Bournemouth to Evercreech Junction* **album contains other views and maps relating to the S&D operations at Templecombe.**

71. The vaulted roof would appear to be a later addition for the benefit of passengers changing trains here. The down platform canopy has no such extension. The carriage and wagon examiner is carrying a long handled hammer used for tapping wheels. A wrong ring would indicate a potential flaw. (Lens of Sutton)

Templecombe	1928	1936
No. of passenger tickets issued	24136	16987
No. of season tickets issued	41	79
No. of tickets collected	28181	24820
No. of telegrams	33616	36182
Parcels forwarded	1352	970
Parcels received	3628	2670
Horses forwarded	88	56
Milk forwarded - cans 1928/gallons1936	24902	218204
Milk received - cans 1928/gallons 1936	6	88
General goods forwarded (tons)	248	152
General goods received (tons)	654	304
Coal, Coke etc.	961	8
Other minerals forwarded	23	4
Other minerals received	2214	42
Trucks livestock forwarded	47	23
Trucks livestock received	61	14
Lavatory pennies	12240	6558

72. The cantilevered platforms from the signal box gave the signalman a view past the canopies and an opportunity for flag signalling. No. 850 was *Lord Nelson*, the first in a class of that name. The trunks may be for boarding-school pupils. (Dr.I.C.Allen)

73. In 1938 the SR totally rebuilt the station, provided a new signal box and an enclosed concrete footbridge. Included in this picture from 29th August 1940 is class K10 4-4-0 no. 138, the new box and much of the marshalling yard. The station was severely bombed on 5th September 1942. (H.C.Casserley)

74. Most of the remainder of the yard is seen in this 1949 portrait of the running-in board. A well wagon appears to be carrying part of a pylon in the days when an endless variety of merchandise could pass the railway observer's eyes. (N.Sprinks)

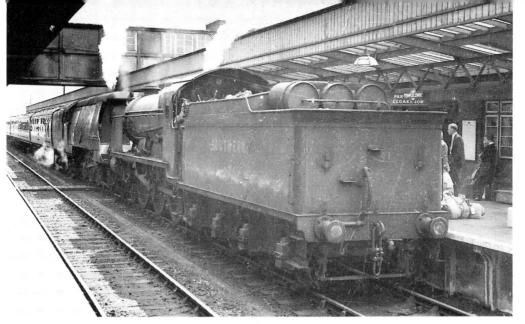

75. The powerful "Merchant Navy" class locomotives were very prone to slipping. On 26th July 1952, no. 35014 *Nederland Line* had reversed the 9.0am from Waterloo along the platform in an attempt to start on the 1 in 150 gradient. Being unsuccessful, class N15x 4-6-0 no. 2331 (still with SR livery) was attached as pilot. There was no shortage of steam for the two mile climb at 1 in 100. (N.Sprinks)

76. Southbound S&D trains (such as the 3.30pm to Bailey Gate seen on 20th September 1952) had to have an engine haul them north to Templecombe No. 2 Junction. It would be detached there - in this case it was ex-LSWR 0395 class 0-6-0 no. 30565. The train engine was class 4 2-6-0 no. 43036. Left is the roof of the former Somerset Central terminus which became the offices of the S&D locomotive depot. (N.Sprinks)

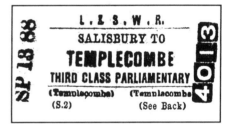

L. & S. W. R.
SP 18 88
SALISBURY TO
TEMPLECOMBE
THIRD CLASS PARLIAMENTARY
4013
(Templecombe)   (Templecombe)
(S.2)   (See Back)

77. Seen in about 1963, no. 34076 *41 Squadron* waits by the down platform water column which was supplied from the tank visible in pictures 76 and 79. The box contained sixty levers, reduced to 16 after the singling. (J.W.T.House/C.L.Caddy)

78. After rebuilding, which included removal of the distinctive boiler casing, the "Merchant Navy" class continued to perform well on the route. No. 35004 *Cunard White Star* accelerates the 1.0pm Waterloo to Plymouth past the goods shed on 24th August 1963. The shed was equipped with a 2-ton crane, freight traffic ceasing on 5th April 1965. (S.C.Nash)

79. The leading coach of the 12.46 Salisbury to Exeter Central is passing over the S&D single line on 31st August 1964, while still rising at 1 in 80. The locomotive is no. 34087 *145 Squadron* and Blackmore Vale forms the background. (J.Scrace)

80. The "Warship" class diesels first ran on the route on 1st August 1964. This is no. D817 *Foxhound*, with the 13.00 Waterloo to Exeter on 5th March 1966, the day before the S&D and Templecombe station closed completely.

Only three of the 130 railway workers here were retained. The population of the village was only about 800 at that time - the community was devastated. (J.N.Faulkner)

TEMPLECOMBE STATION

PROMOTION GROUP

TEMPLECOMBE

SERVING THE BLACKMORE VALE

81. A local committee arranged three party trips in 1982, as the up platform was still usable. This is the scene on 24th July 1983, as no. 50019 makes a special stop with the 18.25 from Exeter St. Davids for another outing. After much agitation, a trial three year reopening commenced on 3rd October 1983. (P.G.Barnes)

London & South Western Ry.

This Ticket is issued subject to the Regulations & Conditions stated in the Company's Time Tables & Bills

WILTON to

TEMPLECOMBE

Wilton to Templecombe	Templecombe to Wilton
3rd CLASS (S.1)	3rd CLASS
Fare 2/1½	Fare 2/1½

4924

82. The result of reopening was an immediate success, proving the folly of closure. Half the upper floor of the signal box was adapted as a waiting room and the signalman issued tickets. A further surprise occurred on 2nd October 1986 when no. 35028 *Clan Line* passed through on a trial run. (S.C.Nash)

83. The platform was weeded and repaired, and seats and lights provided. Seen on 29th July 1987 is the 15.33 Portsmouth Harbour to Sherborne service, worked by DEMU no. 204002. There was one return journey in the afternoons until January 1991, Monday to Fridays only. (V.Mitchell)

84. In 1988 an unrebuilt Bulleid Pacific brought a welcome whiff of steam to the South of England. Working from Salisbury to Yeovil Junction, it is largely obscuring the historic church. The van is at the site of the 1870 bridge for S&D trains. (J.H.Bird)

85. A waiting shelter was added in 1988 as traffic increased. This February 1990 picture shows that a Red Star parcel service, booking facilities and a waiting room were still available in the 1938 signal box. From 1985 to 1991 Templecombe won the annual award for the best kept station in its class on BR. (C.L.Caddy)

86. In 1990 a new building was added to the shelter and a footbridge was erected, from where this photograph of no. 50046 was taken on 10th July 1991. The bridge had previously been in use at Buxted in East Sussex. Note the double track commencing beyond the station and the engineer's siding. The up line is signalled for reversible working to Sherborne. (J.Scrace)

MILBORNE PORT

Milborne Port	1928	1936
No. of passenger tickets issued	7312	4634
No. of season tickets issued	4	15
No. of tickets collected	8821	5588
No. of telegrams	1412	318
Parcels forwarded	2388	3884
Parcels received	3901	5249
Horses forwarded	129	66
Cans of milk forwarded	16407	-
Cans of milk received	13	-
General goods forwarded (tons)	1019	838
General goods received (tons)	1797	1529
Coal, Coke etc.	3740	3066
Other minerals forwarded	56	223
Other minerals received	5236	91
Trucks livestock forwarded	13	2
Trucks livestock received	33	3
Lavatory pennies	-	240

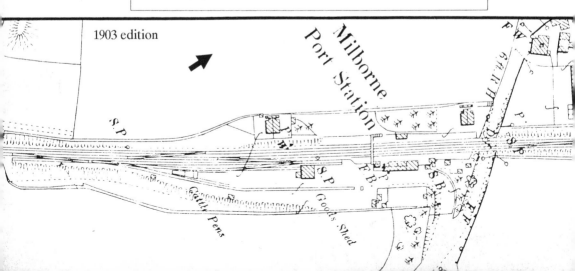

1903 edition

←

87. This is the down side of this typical small LSWR station, and shows the characteristic round headed windows. The signal box dates from July 1875 but the eastern crossover was not added until September 1896. (Lens of Sutton)

88. Co-acting down starting signals were provided, as a single arm could be obscured by the footbridge. Four milk churns are visible on the original print as three porters, the signalman, booking clerk and station master pose for the photographer. (Lens of Sutton)

89. A twelve coach down express speeds down the falling gradient and class N15 no. 456 blows off after the climb from Templecombe on 22nd August 1935. Roof boards are carried by many of the coaches. Expresses such as this were often split to a variety of destinations. (D.Cullum coll.)

90. Two GWR refrigerated vans are behind class K10 no. 145 as it runs through the up platform in 1935. The down starting signal has been repositioned and raised since photograph 88 was taken. (D.Cullum coll.)

91. Two pairs of staff cottages were provided, the other pair showing in picture 89. An up goods is being hauled by Woolwich built class N no. 1854 from 1925. The nearest points to the goods yard were removed in 1949. (D.Cullum coll.)

92. The goods yard closed and station staffing ceased on 6th November 1961. The village of about 1500 souls was one mile south of the station and had an adequate bus service, being on the A30 road. The scene was recorded in July 1962. The house survives as a private dwelling. (C.L.Caddy)

93. In 1960 the steps were repositioned (compare with picture 88) and an area provided in which passengers could pay their fares. From 1961 the offical designation was "Halt" and the notice above the barrow bluntly stated OB-TAIN TICKETS AT SIGNAL BOX. Trains ceased to call on 7th March 1966, the signal box having closed on 21st June 1965, four months before this photograph was taken. (C.L.Caddy)

94. Sherborne Old Castle, and Sherborne Lake beyond it, enhance the backdrop as no.34092 *City of Wells* heads east with the "Blackmoor Vale Express" in July 1988. The lake is fed by the infant River Yeo whose valley the line follows for the remainder of our journey. (J.H.Bird)

95. The famous no.4472 *Flying Scotsman* attacks the gradients of 1 in 100 and 80 east of Sherborne as it returns to Salisbury on 7th June 1987. These beautifully maintained Mk.I first class coaches are used on InterCity Landcruises throughout Britain. (S..C.Nash)

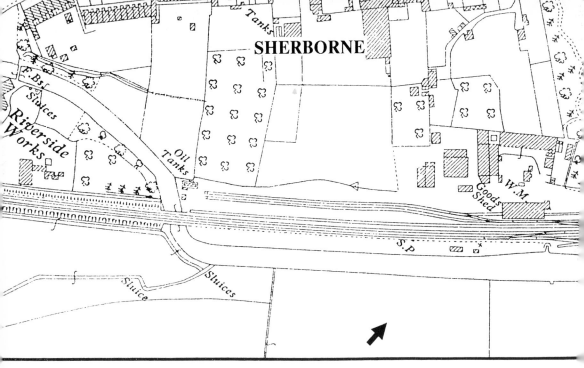

SHERBORNE

96. This important town grew only slowly from 5800 folk when the railway opened to 7200 one hundred years later. A notable trading and manufacturing centre, it had 600 glove makers in 1910. Although the footbridges of lesser stations were enclosed, this remained unglazed. (Lens of Sutton)

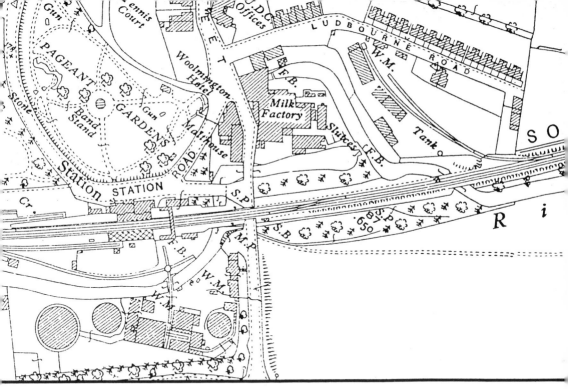

The sidings on the right of this 1901 map were laid down in 1890 to serve the Sherborne Coal & Timber Company, and were later used by Dorset Farmers Ltd. They were lifted in 1965. The nearby milk factory was shown as a silk factory on the 1888 edition.

97. The 1875 signal box is in the background as the staff are recorded. The station master is seated third from the right and the booking clerks sport boaters. (Lens of Sutton)

98. W.H.Smith's bookstall seems well stocked as passengers, perambulators and milk churns wait for an up train. The signal box had 22 levers and a gate wheel. End of term scholars provided peaks in the traffic. There were 400 boys at the famous public school adjacent to the Abbey Church and 250 girls at a younger foundation. (Lens of Sutton)

99. The small River Yeo passed under the line three times within sight of the station. Firstly in the distance and secondly in the foreground. See the left of the map for the third bridge. The small signal arm controlled shunting movements. (Lens of Sutton)

100. U class no.31792 is leaving the goods yard on 9th June 1962, the crane in the background being of 7-ton capacity. The yard closed on 18th April 1966, although it only handled full wagon loads in its final twelve months. "Goodbye Mr.Chips" was filmed here in the early 1960s. (C.L.Caddy)

Sherborne	1928	1936
No. of passenger tickets issued	48169	23612
No. of season tickets issued	67	305
No. of tickets collected	63268	36692
No. of telegrams	5206	2676
Parcels forwarded	35627	31272
Parcels received	32956	38182
Horses forwarded	497	131
Milk forwarded - cans 1928/gallons1936	65888	381851
Milk received - cans 1928/gallons 1936	13	-
General goods forwarded (tons)	4833	1749
General goods received (tons)	11321	9102
Coal, Coke etc.	15028	12762
Other minerals forwarded	606	403
Other minerals received	12451	3870
Trucks livestock forwarded	168	55
Trucks livestock received	99	25
Lavatory pennies	708	1710

101. The canopy seen in the right of picture 98 was replaced by this composite structure in 1962 and DMUs of this type worked some stopping trains from 1964 until 1966. This picture was taken on 16th October 1965 by which time local enterprise was operating the repositioned bookstall - left. (C.L.Caddy)

102. Tite's design was executed in stone from Ham Hill Quarry. This material accounts for the pleasing mellow appearance of many buildings in this attractive part of Dorset. When pictured in 1967 the bookstall had been replaced by a bicycle shed. (J.N.Faulkner)

03. The railway mismanagers of 1967 singled the line from here to Chard Junction on 7th May 1967. They humbly reopened it on 2nd October of the same year, as far as Yeovil Junction, due to the consequent excessive delays. The gasworks (left in this 1970 view) was established in 1836 and was provided with a railway siding over the River Yeo in 1876, the gas company building the bridge. By 1915, 4035 tons of coal was arriving by rail, this increasing to 7000 tons in 1948. Gas making ceased at the end of 1957, when the gas grid from Poole was completed. (C.L.Caddy)

04. A new signal box opened on 18th December 1960, housing 30 levers and a gate wheel. It closed on 4th January 1970 when Yeovil Junction took control of the area and full lifting barriers were installed. These are powered by the station staff and raised by the passage of a train.. No.50050 is arriving with the 11.15 from Waterloo on 30th December 1989, the signals in the distance confirming that the up line is signalled for bidirectional working. (P.G.Barnes)

YEOVIL JUNCTION

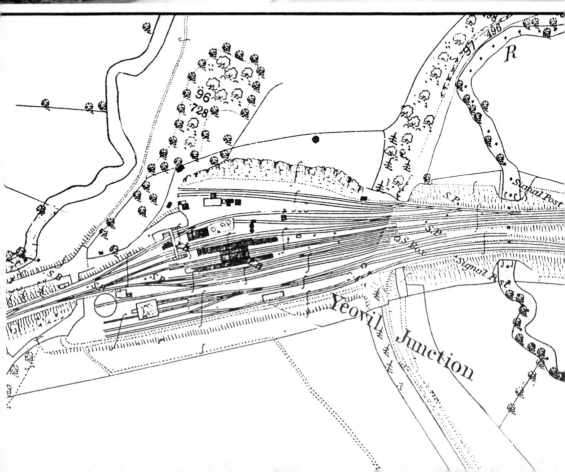

105. The two island platforms date from a major rebuild in 1907-09. Until that time there was only one track between the two islands and through trains were subject to a 20mph limit. Standing on the up through line on 25th May 1935 is class T9 no.283. (H.C.Casserley)

The LSWR Salisbury-Exeter route runs from right to left on this c.1870 map, while the GWR Castle Cary-Dorchester line passes from top right to bottom. The LSWR branch to Yeovil Town is at the rop right corner. The earthworks of the original LSWR line from Sherborne to Yeovil Town are on the right, the bridge over the GWR still being shown although the track was lifted in the 1870s. The GWR's Clifton Maybank branch was in use between June 1864 and June 1937, its function being the transfer of freight between the two companies. Like the GWR main line, it was laid to broad gauge, both being converted to standard gauge in 1874. Note that there are no connections between the systems due to the differing gauges.

L & S.W.R

YEOVIL BRANCH

C.W.R

CLIFTON MAYBANK BRANCH

SALISBURY &

L &

Signal Box

Signal Post

Signal Post

106. On the same day, class N15 4-6-0 no.746 speeds through with the up "Atlantic Coast Express", the most divided train on the SR for many years. Passengers could leave Padstow at 8.35am and arrive at Waterloo at 3.55pm, having had the use of a restaurant car from Exeter Central. (H.C.Casserley)

107. Yeovil "A" Box is in the distance as an up stopping train painted in "blood and custard" livery waits at platform 2. The branch to Yeovil Town passes to the left of the box, the branch train using platform 1. A connection from this branch linked to Yeovil Pen Mill on the former GWR route. (Lens of Sutton)

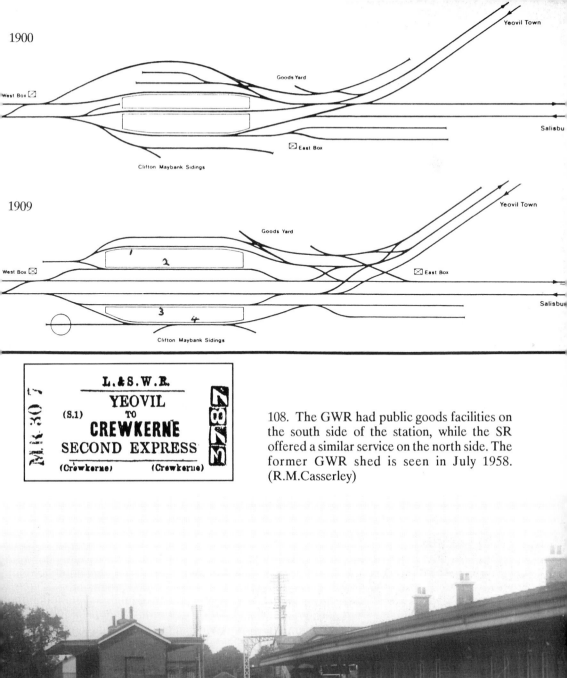

1900

West Box

Goods Yard

Yeovil Town

Salisbu

East Box

Clifton Maybank Sidings

1909

West Box

Goods Yard

Yeovil Town

East Box

Salisbu

Clifton Maybank Sidings

108. The GWR had public goods facilities on the south side of the station, while the SR offered a similar service on the north side. The former GWR shed is seen in July 1958. (R.M.Casserley)

109. In addition to Yeovil Town trains, platform 1 was used by local stopping trains starting here, such as the 12 noon to Salisbury, seen on 14th August 1960. The coaches on the right are Bulleid's early corridor vehicles and the locomotive is a class S15 4-6-0, no.30831. (E.Wilmshurst)

110. A westward view from the end of platforms 1 and 2 in about 1962 reveals that there was no direct access to platform 1. This was not possible until 26th March 1975. "B" Box (right) was closed on 30th April 1967 and for the ensuing eight years only one platform was used. The locomotive is no.34003 *Plymouth*. (C.L.Caddy)

Yeovil Junction	1928	1936
No. of passenger tickets issued	20376	15358
No. of season tickets issued	64	22
No. of tickets collected	24334	21105
No. of telegrams	2795	4259
Parcels forwarded	474	342
Parcels received	1133	722
Horses forwarded	41	14
Milk forwarded - cans 1928/gallons1936	159	93710
Cans of milk received	10	-
General goods forwarded (tons)	40	56
General goods received (tons)	790	201
Coal, Coke etc.	38	22
Other minerals forwarded	75	16
Other minerals received	2222	1515
Trucks livestock forwarded	50	12
Trucks livestock received	14	6
Lavatory pennies	1128	2469

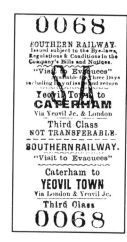

111. After transfer to the Western Region in 1963, the Yeovil Town service was often worked by ex-GWR stock. This applied on 4th July 1964, when 0-6-0PT no.6435 was coupled to an auto trailer, elsewhere known as a push-pull coach. (E.Wilmshurst)

112. Having taken water, class M7 0-4-4T no.30131 waits at platform 1 with the Yeovil Town service on 28th April 1962. Arriving at platform 3 is the 12 noon departure for Exeter Central which will call at all stations. (E.Wilmshurst)

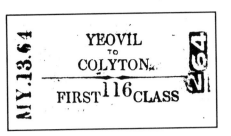

113. Following the withdrawal in September 1964 of all services from Waterloo to destinations west of Exeter, the Western Region provided a through Saturday train from Paddington to Ilfracombe for the 1965 season. To avoid reversal at Exeter St.Davids this ran via Castle Cary, Yeovil Junction and Exeter Central. Hymek D7072 brings this train into Yeovil Junction off the connection from Pen Mill on 7th August 1965. (J.N.Faulkner)

114. Before the branch service to Yeovil Town was withdrawn on 2nd October 1966 it had been reduced to a railbus shuttle. Here W79976 built by AC Cars of Thames Ditton leaves Yeovil Junction on 7th August 1965. Following this withdrawal, a shuttle service to Pen Mill was operated until 4th May 1968. (J.N.Faulkner)

115. Engineering work on the WR main line near Taunton on 30th March 1985 resulted in diversion of Paddington - West of England services. Consequently Waterloo trains terminated here and locomotives accumulated. No. 33025 is departing for Brighton while cars wait on wagons on the right. (P.G.Barnes)

London & South Western Ry.
This Ticket is issued subject to the Regulations
& Conditions stated in the Company's Time
Tables & Bills
SALISBURY to
YEOVIL
Via Yeovil Junc.
Salisbury   Salisbury
Yeovil   Yeovil
3rd CLASS   (S.6)   3rd CLASS
Fare 3/4   Fare 3/4

116. On the same day, no. 50042 is seen from the same location, arriving from Paddington. Tyer's electric train staff has been used to Pen Mill since the line was singled on 26th May 1968. Tokenless block working applies on the main line. (P.G.Barnes)

117. The 70ft vacuum operated turntable was retained for turning engineer's equipment but returned to its original use when steam specials were introduced in 1986. This 1988 view shows passengers on platform 3 - another rare occurrence as its footbridge had been removed. (J.H.Bird) WRONG. PLTFM 3 ON STATION. THIS WAS OLD ENGINEERS PLTFM.

118. From 1968 until 1988 passengers were expected to make their own way between Yeovil's two stations and to the town. A minibus service subsequently met their need and is seen on 16th April 1990. The booking office and privately operated buffet are on the platform. (V.Mitchell)

0490

SOUTHERN RAILWAY.
Issued subject to the Bye-laws,
Regulations & Conditions in the
Company's Bills and Notices.
H.M.F. on LEAVE.
Bristol(Temple Meads)to
DINTON
Via G.W. & Salisbury
Third Class
NOT TRANSFERABLE.

SOUTHERN RAILWAY
H.M.F. on LEAVE.

Dinton
Bristol(T.M.)
Dinton to
BRISTOL
(TEMPLE MEADS)
Via Salisbury & G.W.R.
Third Class

0490

> Other maps and photographs of this area can be seen in our *Yeovil to Exeter* and *Yeovil to Dorchester* albums.

0041

SOUTHERN RAILWAY
RACES
Available as advertised
Epsom to
YEOVIL TOWN
Via Waterloo
Third Class
FOR CONDITIONS
SEE BACK

SOUTHERN RAILWAY
RACES
Available as advertised
Yeovil Town
Epsom
Yeovil Town to
EPSOM
Via Waterloo
Third Class

0041

119. Apart from coal traffic which continued to arrive from Didcot occasionally, goods services were withdrawn on 5th April 1965. Repainted blue and bearing its original number of D400 for sentimental reasons, this class 50 diesel is running round the stock of the 18.30 departure for Waterloo on 18th May 1991. The last of the class was withdrawn 12 months later. (P.G.Barnes)

120. Diversion of Paddington services (left) was necessary again on 18th May 1991 and so the 11.14 Southampton to Plymouth had to be terminated here, no. 50037 being seen running round it. This useful Saturdays-only train had started at Brighton and run via Portsmouth Harbour until January of that year. After suffering the unreliability of ageing diesel locomotives for many years, hopes were high that improvements would result from the introduction of 22 class 159 Sprinters in 1993, the first new stock on the route for over 40 years. (P.G.Barnes)

MP Middleton Press

Easebourne Lane, Midhurst. West Sussex. GU29 9AZ
Tel: (0730) 813169   Fax: (0730) 812601
Write or telephone for our latest booklist

BRANCH LINES

BRANCH LINES TO MIDHURST
BRANCH LINES AROUND MIDHURST
BRANCH LINES TO HORSHAM
BRANCH LINE TO SELSEY
BRANCH LINES TO EAST GRINSTEAD
BRANCH LINES TO ALTON
BRANCH LINE TO TENTERDEN
BRANCH LINES TO NEWPORT
BRANCH LINES TO TUNBRIDGE WELLS
BRANCH LINE TO SWANAGE
BRANCH LINE TO LYME REGIS
BRANCH LINE TO FAIRFORD
BRANCH LINE TO ALLHALLOWS
BRANCH LINES AROUND ASCOT
BRANCH LINES AROUND WEYMOUTH
BRANCH LINE TO HAWKHURST
BRANCH LINES AROUND EFFINGHAM JN
BRANCH LINE TO MINEHEAD
BRANCH LINE TO SHREWSBURY
BRANCH LINES AROUND HUNTINGDON
BRANCH LINES TO SEATON AND SIDMOUTH
BRANCH LINES AROUND WIMBORNE
BRANCH LINES TO EXMOUTH
BRANCH LINE TO LYNTON
BRANCH LINE TO SOUTHWOLD

SOUTH COAST RAILWAYS

CHICHESTER TO PORTSMOUTH
BRIGHTON TO EASTBOURNE
RYDE TO VENTNOR
EASTBOURNE TO HASTINGS
HASTINGS TO ASHFORD
SOUTHAMPTON TO BOURNEMOUTH
ASHFORD TO DOVER
BOURNEMOUTH TO WEYMOUTH
DOVER TO RAMSGATE

COUNTRY RAILWAY ROUTES

BOURNEMOUTH TO EVERCREECH JN
READING TO GUILDFORD
WOKING TO ALTON
BATH TO EVERCREECH JUNCTION
GUILDFORD TO REDHILL
EAST KENT LIGHT RAILWAY
FAREHAM TO SALISBURY
BURNHAM TO EVERCREECH JUNCTION
REDHILL TO ASHFORD
YEOVIL TO DORCHESTER
ANDOVER TO SOUTHAMPTON

SOUTHERN MAIN LINES

HAYWARDS HEATH TO SEAFORD
EPSOM TO HORSHAM
CRAWLEY TO LITTLEHAMPTON
THREE BRIDGES TO BRIGHTON
WATERLOO TO WOKING
VICTORIA TO EAST CROYDON
EAST CROYDON TO THREE BRIDGES
WOKING TO SOUTHAMPTON
WATERLOO TO WINDSOR
LONDON BRIDGE TO EAST CROYDON
BASINGSTOKE TO SALISBURY
SITTINGBOURNE TO RAMSGATE
YEOVIL TO EXETER
CHARING CROSS TO ORPINGTON
VICTORIA TO BROMLEY SOUTH
ORPINGTON TO TONBRIDGE
FAVERSHAM TO DOVER

LONDON SUBURBAN RAILWAYS

CHARING CROSS TO DARTFORD
HOLBORN VIADUCT TO LEWISHAM
KINGSTON & HOUNSLOW LOOPS
CRYSTAL PALACE AND CATFORD LOOP
LEWISHAM TO DARTFORD
MITCHAM JUNCTION LINES

STEAMING THROUGH

STEAMING THROUGH EAST HANTS
STEAMING THROUGH SURREY
STEAMING THROUGH WEST SUSSEX
STEAMING THROUGH THE ISLE OF WIGHT
STEAMING THROUGH WEST HANTS

OTHER RAILWAY BOOKS

GARRAWAY FATHER & SON
LONDON CHATHAM & DOVER RAILWAY
INDUSTRIAL RAILWAYS OF THE S. EAST
WEST SUSSEX RAILWAYS IN THE 1980s
SOUTH EASTERN RAILWAY

OTHER BOOKS

TILLINGBOURNE BUS STORY
MILITARY DEFENCE OF WEST SUSSEX
BATTLE OVER SUSSEX 1940
SURREY WATERWAYS
KENT AND EAST SUSSEX WATERWAYS
HAMPSHIRE WATERWAYS